Overcoming the 3 D's

Depression
Discouragement
Despair

Jim Ayer

Remnant Publications

Coldwater MI 49036
www.remnantpublications.com

Copyright © 2008
by Jim Ayer
All Rights Reserved
Printed in the USA

Published by
Remnant Publications
649 East Chicago Road
Coldwater MI 49036
517-279-1304
www.remnantpublications.com

Edited by Debi Tesser
Cover design by David Berthiaume
Text design by Greg Solie • AltamontGraphics.com

ISBN: 978-1-933291-31-4

Overcoming the 3Ds
Depression, Discouragement, Despair

On the other end of the phone was a friend of mine, who is also my publisher, and during our conversation, he asked me if I would pray about writing a book on discouragement and depression. My first response was, "Well, I'm not sure I'm the one that should write a book on the subject. Of course, I've had some real down times in my life that could have caused me problems, but I try not to let that happen. I usually bounce back fairly quickly."

"That's why I think you should write the book," he responded. "I've seen how you react to very difficult situations and trials. You sing, you praise the Lord, and you deal with them in a very positive way." "OK, I see your point; I'll pray about it and let you know," I responded.

The rest of the day I couldn't rid my mind of our discussion. The idea intrigued me, but I had no idea where to begin writing or if that was the direction God wanted me to take. But then, like a bolt of lightening—a small one—I thought about the two frogs. Two frogs? Yes, two frogs.

I read a book some time ago and found a poem whose author is apparently unknown. But being the country boy I am, I just loved it. I want to share it with you:

> Two frogs fell into a can of cream, or so it's been told.
> The sides of the can were shiny and steep; the cream was deep and cold.
> "O, what's the use," said number one, "Tis fate; no help's around."
> "Good-bye my friend! Good-bye, cruel world." And weeping still, he drowned.
> But number two of sterner stuff, dog-paddled in surprise,
> And he licked his creamy lips and blinked his creamy eyes.
> I'll swim awhile at least, he thought, or so it has been said.
> It really couldn't help the world if one more frog were dead.
> An hour or more he kicked and swam, not once did he stop to mutter
> Then he hopped out—on a mound of fresh-churned butter!

Did you notice? Did you catch it? This poem is why I decided to share my ideas on the 3Ds. Think about it for a moment. Aside from the poem being cute—at least in my opinion—what else do you see?

This is what created the "Ah-ha" moment for me: both frogs had fallen into the very same shiny, steep-sided, can of deep, cold cream. They were both stuck and held prisoner by the same set of circumstances, and the outcome did not look good from the vantage point of either frog.

"Wow, there it is!" My friend was right, and led by the Lord, I decided to write this booklet. Now in case you are still wondering what on earth I'm talking about, I realized that, in this world of sin and suffering, everyone has "fiery trials" as Peter refers to them, "Beloved, think it not strange concerning the fiery trial which is to try you, as though some strange thing happened unto you: But rejoice, inasmuch as ye are partakers of Christ's sufferings; that, when his glory shall be revealed, ye may be glad also with exceeding joy" (1 Peter 4:12, 13).

We are all in the same world, and there is nothing "no new thing under the sun" (Ecclesiastes 1:9). But what makes the difference is how we react to the fiery trials that assault us on a daily basis.

Under the weight of the cold cream trial, frog number one decided to give up and die, but afflicted with the same trial, trapped in the same bucket, the second frog decided to put his energies into staying afloat for at "least a while." It was all about perspective.

What Condition Your Condition Is In

Rabbi Stephen Pearce shared an interesting story about Nazi hunter Simon Wiesenthal. He "had been haunted by a troubling event from his youth when he was interned in a concentration camp. He observed that there was only one prayer book in the camp, and he was offended that the man who owned it would only let people pray from it if they gave him a portion of their meager food allowance.

"Once, when Wiesenthal told this story to a rabbi to explain why he wasn't religious, the rabbi asked Wiesenthal, 'Why do you focus so much on what that selfish, manipulative man did and not make note of what all the other people did? Aren't you impressed that people who were starving would be willing to give up some of their precious food allowance in order to hold a prayer book in their hands for even a few minutes?' Wiesenthal realized that he had focused only on the greed of one man and not on the piety, faith and sacrifice of so many others" (Rabbi Stephen Pearce, "Angry Giants or

'Good Land'? Fears Still Can Incapacitate," *The Jewish News Weekly*, Friday, June 7, 2002).

Perspective is an interesting mental location. From its vantage point humans ascend to the mountain tops or plummet to the depths.

In 1968, Kenny Rogers sang these words in hit song "Just Dropped In," "I just dropped in to see what condition my condition was in." That was the name I was always intrigued by the song because I thought it had a real-life application. In what condition is your condition? Are you discouraged and starting to sink while those around you seem to be paddling their way to the safety of the butter mound? Have you reached the point of depression and heading down to the depths of despair? If so, read on dear reader because there is hope for you!

I'm sure you have heard the old adage, "Misery loves company." I doubt that there is anyone who would disagree that a "pity party" is a very popular gathering—and usually very well attended. According to a 2007 study by the World Health Organization and Harvard Medical School, 9.6 percent of Americans suffer from bipolar disorder, major depressive disorder, or chronic minor depression over the course of a year.

Interestingly, depression is more common in the rich and affluent. I have seen people in areas of the world so poor that a riot would almost erupt over the desire to possess a single, discarded paint can, and yet they were happy people—so money, power, and fame are not the answer.

Pilgrim's Progress

Make no mistake about it—everyone has problems. We are in a sinful world with a real devil who wants to destroy us using whatever means he can. That's what caused John Bunyan, in his book *Pilgrim's Progress*, to write about Christian.

Christian was a traveler who became mired in the Slough of Despond. He slipped into the slough because he lacked a commitment to God, associated with the wrong friends, and led a deficient prayer life. Giant Despair captured a miserable Christian and took him to Doubting Castle where he eventually was expected to commit suicide.

As he endured the horrible ordeal, he suddenly realized he still had the Key of Hope, which was called Promise. He finally remembered that the Key of Promise would unlock all the locked doors of Doubting Castle.

This is the exciting part of the story for you and me. Christian used the Key of Hope and finally escaped the enemy's camp … he never looked back. The promises of God are powerful and will set us free! And listen to this: The wounds Christian sustained were healed by God with the leaves from the Tree of Life.

The devil wants each and every one of us to become trapped in the muck and mire of the Slough of Despond. Once we are stuck in the Slough, the devil gets very excited as he unleashes the Giant Despair on us … or as we are discussing here: the 3Ds. How do troubled and discouraged people, including myself, handle and overcome troubles and fiery trials?

Happy As You Choose to Be

If there has ever been a man who had a right to be depressed or worse, it was Abraham Lincoln. He had good reason to suffer from the 3Ds … and he did for a time. This was a man who lost his fiancée, a man who never won an election until he finally won the presidency, and then the entire nation began to unravel before his very eyes into civil war. His own party attacked him. The Copperheads, those who thought he should compromise on slavery, gave him great grief, and the Radical

Republicans thought he was too slow to abolish slavery. He was the president of a nation ripped apart during the worst of nightmares, but Lincoln still overcame.

How? I believe he had a grasp on the Almighty and clung to His promises. I believe this allowed him to make the statement that both he and I have chosen to adopt into our lives: "Most people are about as happy as they choose to be."

Some people may say that Lincoln was simply trying to raise himself by his own shoelaces, but remember what the Bible says, "Choose you this day whom you will serve" (Joshua 24:15). We do have a choice, and the choices we make have eternal consequences.

This little-known information may offer a sharp point to the thought of eternal consequences. During his watch just before midnight on April 14, 1912, Charles Groves, the ship's third officer on the ocean-liner California, was on his top deck and saw the lights of another ship rapidly passing his own on a westward course. As it did, he saw a beautiful display of lights, which revealed a large passenger liner. Suddenly, it seemed that the huge liner abruptly stopped and extinguished most of her lights. It didn't occur to him that the lights were still lit but they had only appeared to go out because the ship was no longer broadside but had swerved radically to the left.

That night, even though help was not far away, more than 1,500 people lost their lives in one of history's worst shipping disasters … because of no communication. Help was very near, but there had been no communication. So when the mighty Titanic sank, nobody was there to help.

Speaking of the spiritual realm, many people are drowning when help is near … the help of God, the help of the church, and the help of friends and acquaintances.

You may be tempted to say … or you might be saying right now, "I'm just wired differently." "I can't help my despair." "My depression can't be helped." "I am a melancholy personality. "It's in my genes." "I was born that way, and I can't change." "I always see the glass as half empty." "If I was stuck in the can of cream, I know I would be frog number one that quit and drowned."

The War

If we were in this world alone, I would fully agree with you, but we are not here alone. The reason we feel like we may feel one of the 3Ds is that we are in a war—a war between good and evil. "Be sober, be vigilant; because your adversary the devil, as a roaring lion, walketh about, seeking whom he may devour" (1 Peter 5:8). It's a spiritual war, and it's a mental war. But make no mistake about it—IT IS A REAL WAR! You must make the decision and personal choice that you do not want to be a causality of this war—because help is very near.

Good. If you are reading this paragraph, I assume that you wish to continue to discover how others have chosen to seek the help that is freely offered by God and apply those principles to your life right now.

Through his servant John, the Lord revealed to us, "Beloved, I wish above all things that thou mayest prosper and be in health, even as thy soul prospereth" (3 John 1:2).

Again, in the book of Jeremiah He shared these exciting promises … promises for you and me: "For I know the thoughts that I think toward you, saith the LORD, thoughts of peace, and not of evil, *to give you an expected end.* Then shall ye call upon me, and ye shall go and pray unto me, and I will hearken unto you. *And ye shall seek me, and find me*, when ye shall search for me with all your heart" (Jeremiah 29:11-13, emphasis supplied).

Just as declared in the preceding verses, every thought God has toward us is good. Think about this. No matter what happens in your life, God settled His love for you on Calvary's cross. Every trial, every challenge that causes you to feel like you are in the can with the frogs must be viewed against the backdrop of the cross, which is our starting point for success and victory over the 3Ds.

You may ask, "If God loves me so much and cares so deeply for me then why do I suffer under the weight of one or more of the 3Ds?" The answer has already been revealed. The mask of Satan has been ripped away. "Be sober, be vigilant; because your adversary the devil, as a roaring lion, walketh about, seeking whom he may devour" (1 Peter 5:8).

Lessons from a Jail Cell

Just as our Father loves us, the devil hates us, and that hatred drives his all consuming passion … to destroy every human on this planet.

Like the jailer at Philippi when the earthquake struck, we must ask, "What must I do to be saved?" The answer is that we must learn from those who have gone before us and have gained the victory. Speaking of Philippi, let's look at the surrounding story.

Paul and Silas traveled to the city of Philippi to take the good news of Christ to all who would listen. During their stay, they activated the power of God and cast a demon from a woman tormented and possessed by the devil. This caused a great stir among those who had been making a living from this poor captive of the devil. So much of a stir that the mob ripped the clothes from Paul and Silas, beat them, and then threw them into prison. What did they do? They sang. Yes, we are told that their singing was so mighty that God hurled an earthquake that jolted the foundation of the prison, flung open every prison door, and unfastened the prisoners' chains. I would call that good singing! (See Acts 16:11-40.)

Have you ever tried it? Have you ever tried singing away your blues? You should because God says, "A merry heart doeth good like a medicine" (Proverbs 17:22). I would submit to you that you don't even need to sing very well … just with a heart wanting to reach to God. May I suggest a tune for you? It's one that I have enjoyed. It's called, "Turn Your Eyes upon Jesus."

It goes something like this (oh that's right you can't hear me sing … just as well I guess). "Turn your eyes upon Jesus, look full in His wonderful face; and the things of earth will grow strangely dim in the light of His glory and grace." How true and wonderful are these words.

Speaking of Paul, it is hard to imagine what he endured, and yet he could still raise his voice in joyful song to the Lord. In 2 Corinthians 11, he shared that he had been beaten three times with rods, stoned, shipwrecked three times, and spent a day in the sea. This does not include being cast into prison to languish there for the sake of the gospel. And these were not prisons with television sets, DVDs, and workout rooms.

The Apostle Paul, however, was fighting the good fight of faith. He knew that by grasping with all of his might onto the promises of his Lord, God would sustain him.

John's Example?

Not all of the Lord's followers have been so steadfast in their walk. One who faltered may surprise you—John the Baptist. You may know most of John's story. He was chosen to herald the coming of Christ. He was extremely faithful in his calling, including his announcement to the growing crowd that Jesus stood among them. And the crown jewel of his ministry was to baptize Jesus.

But then something happened … He was thrown into prison for telling Herod, the governor, that his involvement with his brother's wife must end. As John languished in the darkness of his prison cell, he allowed his mind to run wild with speculation. When we allow these kinds of thoughts to go unchecked, our minds become the devil's playground. Soon this man of God had his own moment with the 3Ds. You can read the actual account in Matthew 11.

John raised himself from the filth of the dungeon floor. Grasping the cold metal bars he shoved his face toward his disciples speaking these, almost, callous words, "Is he the one or do we look for another?" (Matthew 11:3, author's paraphrase).

From the time he announced that Jesus was the Christ to this awful moment, we see the erosion of a man's faith because he lost his focus on God. He began looking at his dismal surroundings. He did not keep his mind fixed on God; instead, John allowed his surroundings to affect his belief in, and walk with, the Father.

Before you think that all was lost, we must finish the story. When John's disciples posed this question to Jesus, he did not scold them. What He did do was share words that were designed to not only encourage John and his disciples but also to encourage you and me.

"Jesus answered and said unto them, Go and show John again those things which ye do hear and see. The blind receive their sight, and the lame walk, the lepers are cleansed, and the deaf hear, the dead are raised up, and the poor have the gospel preached to them. And blessed is he, whosoever shall not be offended in me" (Matthew 11:5, 6).

Notice that Jesus delivered this powerfully good news, and then he gave John just a slight tap on the wrist by saying "How happy are those who have no doubts about me!" (Matthew 11:6, *Good News Bible*). This news is equally powerful for you and for me.

Jesus seemed to be saying, "John, don't get sidetracked by circumstances. Keep focused on me. See who I really am. I am the Creator God of the universe who raises the dead and has power to do everything! Don't let Satan get to you. Yes, your prison cell is dark, stinking, damp, and the rats are vile, but I am with you, and I will turn your despair into victory. Trust in me! Keep looking at me and nothing else!

After the disciples left the area, He told the crowd that John was the greatest of all prophets. This is encouraging because, to me, it meant that John overcame the 3Ds and took courage prior to his life being abruptly ended.

Peter: From the Brink and Back

Let's look at another story of hope. It's the story of Peter; the disciple often pompously expressed his own opinions. Peter always had something to say about everything ... even when it was inappropriate.

Just before Jesus' great test of faith Jesus in the Garden of Gethsemane, He told Peter that he would deny Him three times. In his usual over-the-top behavior, Peter said that he would never do such a thing, but it wasn't long before the evening found Peter huddled next to a fire in the very courtyard very near to where Jesus was being tried for crimes He did not commit.

Soon identified by those who sat around the same fire as a close follower of Christ, Peter blurted the words of denial, then anger, and finally he burst into the rant of a fisherman's cursing. With the words still dripping from his lips like thick slime, he heard the crystal clear call of the prophetic rooster.

In that moment he saw the Savior and realized that everything Jesus had told him was true. He was not the pillar of strength he thought he was, and he had denied His Lord with cursing and swearing.

His heart was broken as he ran from the courtyard in shame—wishing he could die. You can't get much lower in the 3Ds than Peter was at that moment. This is exactly where the devil wanted Peter, and it's where he wants us … well, let me correct that … he wants us to go the last step and end it all just like Judas did.

God could have glossed over this part of the biblical account, but He didn't because it's another story of hope, love, and direction for you and me. But you say, "How can that be?" Let's continue.

Both disciples suffered tremendous pain because each of them betrayed Christ, and they were reeling under the weight of self condemnation, guilt, and despair. But one of them did not give up, and the payoff was huge!

Judas chose to throw away eternal happiness for momentary relief. You see, God created us for eternity not just for time. Don't downplay the significance of this statement. Judas opted for temporary relief from this brief blip of time, so now he will miss indescribable joy of forever!

On the other hand, Peter was wracked with mental anguish and unimaginable trauma caused by denying the Son of God; I believe he clung to the previous, precious time he spent with Jesus. Because of this, he was better able to weather the storm until the Son shown through the storm clouds (notice the play on sun?).

Go Tell Peter

On Sunday morning, Mary and the other women went to the tomb to anoint the body of Jesus but what they found were only grave clothes and two men in white apparel. One instructed Mary to go and "tell his disciples and Peter" (Mark 16:7) that the Lord has risen. I just love this part of the story.

The angel first said to her to go and tell everyone that the Lord has risen, but then he added Peter by name ... don't forget to tell Peter. Whatever you do, tell Peter that the Lord still loves him. Get rid of the 3Ds! It's not as bad as you think it is Peter. Every dark day has its dawn. I was dead and now I'm alive, and I love you! Put your trust in Me, and you will get past this.

Please forgive me for what some may consider irreverence, but, to me, this is the frogs-in-the-can story incognito. Judas is frog number one who let the 3Ds overcome him and gave up too soon. Peter is frog number two who decided to paddle a while and finally walked from his "sure death" experience to again look into the face of His God and live.

The Barney Fife Method

There is a story of a lady who had a dream that she and a friend were in a beautiful garden. As they were passing through the beauty with the owner of the garden, her friend began to complain about the thorns and thistles that were impeding the pathway. She found a deformed tree and a stunted rosebush. The Guide instructed her to follow Him and to keep her focus upon Him and that she should gather the beautiful lilies, the pinks, and the roses (*Steps to Christ*, pp. 116-117).

Have you noticed that all of our stories have the same theme? This is how Abraham Lincoln, John the Baptist, the Apostle Peter, and even I find the strength to overcome what usually starts as discouragement, can lead to depression, and tumble down to utter despair.

When I was young, I used to watch a TV show call *The Andy Griffith Show*. The storyline took place in the town of Mayberry where Sheriff Andy Taylor and his trusty, bumbling Deputy Barney Fife would deal with all sorts of problems. What I loved most was Barney and his comical antics. He had a great saying that I think has some good religion in it.

If you have ever watched the show, do you remember what he saying was? "We've got to nip it in the bud, Andy! We've go to nip it in the bud." Yes, indeed, a lot of religion in it.

When Barney came across a perceived problem, he wanted to act on it immediately before things got out of hand. That's what you and I must do, or we will end up like frog number one. Certainly, frog number two had the preferred outcome.

Don't miss this point. All of us experience disappointment in our lives. We all have thorns and thistles. But if we don't "nip it in the bud," these things can lead to depression, which, if left unchecked, can lead downward to despair.

How Do We Fight Back?

Now buckle your seat belt and hang on because I'm going to give you several pointers in rapid-fire succession to help you paddle. It's time to make butter so you can climb from the can in which you may be trapped.

The first thing I would like you to do is start your day, every day, by writing 10 things in praise to God. I learned this from a fellow many years ago by the name of Glenn Coon. He said, "If you can't think of anything to praise the Lord about, then try holding your breath for five minutes and then see if you can think of anything." This may be a hard exercise at first, but start "paddling," and it will become easier as your praise muscles strengthen.

The question is, "What do I mean by paddle since we cannot save ourselves?" Let me explain. You have a will that makes choices independently from God. He created you that way because He loves you. He can do nothing in you unless you allow him to do so; by laying all the desires of self aside, God can give you the strength to paddle. This is where Paul gained his victory. He called it dying to self and giving his will to God. In order to overcome the 3Ds that plague your life, you must remember to focus upon the Guide and not the thorns. This choice of will you can, and must, make.

An old preacher was alone in the chapel on his knees before the pulpit. His conversation went something like this: "Lord, yesterday I tied up all my problems and trials, and I gave them to you. Today, Father, I promise to give them all to you again, but this time I am also going to give you the string that I was hanging onto yesterday."

You must let go of life if you are to live. This may be a radical thought for you but you are the one to choose between life and death.

There used to be a sign posted on the Alaska Highway that read: "Choose your rut carefully; you will be in it for the next 200 miles." Since I was born and raised in snow country, this sign meant a great deal to me. As the snow falls, it becomes deeper and deeper. As the cars and trucks make their way along the roadway, the snow ruts gets deeper and deeper as well … so deep, in fact, that soon you can't seem to get out of the track that you are in because you are stuck in a one-direction rut.

Don't fall for the devil's lies like Judas and frog number one. God is close by. He loves you and is waiting to lift you from that rut at this very moment. Nevertheless, He expects you to expend some energy. Reach up to Him, and cry out for His help, or to put it plainly—paddle!

The second thing I suggest is a paddle that I call the back stroke. I guarantee that it will be life-changing … it was for me. Are you ready for it? Back away from the television set. That's right, shut it off and stop gathering the thorns, the thistles, and all of the other garbage on TV. Most of what is on nowadays was neither designed to help you overcome the 3Ds, nor was it designed with the goal of helping you live a happy productive life ... now or in the world to come. Start by giving it a try for a week. Read your Bible instead. Go for a walk in a quiet park. Start to refocus your mind.

Here's a third suggestion: Seek a neighbor or someone in your church family who needs some help, any help, and go help them. Many people are dying without Christ in their lives, so go fulfill your part of the Gospel Commission, and share Jesus with them. I know it sounds radical, but it will transform your life. Shift your mind from yourself to them. John the Baptist was doing just fine when he was helping others find Jesus Christ. Only when he focused on his own problems did his troubles begin.

In 1974, a study in Alameda, California, conducted by Lisa Berkman, Ph.D., with 7,000 people, found that those who had extensive social ties had death rates two to three times lower than those who were isolated. A study with 2,750 patients at the University of Michigan experienced the same results. Take some time to get out and make friends! As Phil Callaway said, "Even the ants have time to attend picnics."

The fourth suggestion stems from the training techniques. Every swimmer must go into training in order to build strength. Here are some training tips that will make a significant difference in your mental outlook and paddling ability. You may want to consult your physician before changing certain dietary habits.

1. *Get physical exercise.* Now that you have shut off the TV, enjoy the sunshine, and go for a walk. The sun is a great mood enhancer.

2. *Awaken and go to bed at the same time* seven days a week. Scientists have found that your sleep patterns will improve greatly by this habit, which in turn will help your outlook on life.

3. *Get eight hours of sleep*, then get up; don't lay around in bed.

4. *Avoid all caffeinated beverages.*

5. *Cut down on refined sugar* and processed sweets, and eat more fresh fruits in their place.

6. *Eat only three meals each day*, and do not eat snacks in between meals unless your doctor says otherwise.

Order in your life: God is a God of order. Before you proceed to the next set of practices think about this one a while. Most people spend more time planning their vacation than they do the rest of their lives.

Each night before you go to bed, create a "to-do list" for the following day. List the items of highest priority first, and make a list with the least important last. Also, make the list with only those things you can complete in a day because too many items will be overwhelming. As you strengthen your organizational skills, you may add additional items. In the morning start at the top of your list and work your way down the list crossing off the completed items. This practice will give you great satisfaction, which in turn means a happier mental attitude. If you experience interruptions during the day, and we all do, get back to your list as soon as you can. At the end of the day, assess your list and start the new one for the following day, beginning with the most important items first.

High-priority Practices for Overcoming the 3Ds

A) *Praise the Lord*—Start the habit of finding something during the day for which to thank the Lord … out loud! Proverbs 12:25 says, "Anxiety in a man's heart weighs him down, but a good word makes him glad" (English Standard Version). Praise Him for what you do have. We worry about what we don't have rather than being happy for what we do have.

B) *Sing*—When the way gets harder, sing a happy song. Remember, "a merry heart doeth good like a medicine" (Proverbs 17:22). One of my personal favorites was an old Walt Disney song:

"Zip-a-dee-do-dah, zip-a-de-ay,
 My, oh my, what a wonderful day.
 Plenty of sunshine headin' my way.
 Zip-a-dee-do-dah, zip-a-de-ay!

"Mr. Bluebird's on my shoulder,
 It's the truth, it's actual,
 Everything is satisfactual!

"Zip-a-dee-do-dah, zip-a-de-ay,
  Wonderful feelin', wonderful day!"

I can testify to the fact that it is hard to be even remotely discouraged when singing that song.

C) *Memorize Scripture*—Start memorizing Bible promises, and recite them when you are tempted with despondency. Jesus beat the devil with this practice.

D) *Study the Word and Pray*—Samuel Chadwick said, "There is no way to learn to pray but by praying."

If you or I ever hope to overcome the 3Ds, we must spend time in the God's Word and in prayer. At the beginning of Christ's public ministry, and after 40 days in the desert, the devil hit him hard. But Jesus quoted scripture, and it left the devil speechless. It was not hand-to-hand combat that beat him, but it was the power in knowing the Word of God.

At the close of His mission, Jesus faced the devil again—on the way to the cross, in the Garden of Gethsemane. The Garden is where he gained the final victory. I say final because he spent years in study and on His knees in prayer to the Father gaining strength for this battle … and now this was it … the ultimate test to see if humanity would survive.

What young man in his early thirties wants to die? If anyone might have had a problem with the 3Ds, Jesus could have. He didn't want to die, and three times he cried out to the Father to let the trial pass from Him. Three times He did exactly what you and I must do to win our battles over discouragement, depression, and despair—He bundled every promise of the Father's, he remembered every conversation they had ever shared, and then he said, "Not my will, Father, but your will."

You can do this! The same power that was available to Jesus enabling Him to surrender his will to beat the devil and overcome the cross is yours. Do not abandon hope. By God's power, you will walk on fresh-churned butter into the glorious light of the first day of eternity.

When you look around, you will shout Hallelujah!

I'm here, and Heaven is cheap enough!

The trials and troubles that you faced on earth will be as nothing in comparison to the glories of the New Earth. Yes, yes, keep paddling because your journey is but a short one, and you can do it!

With Jesus by your side, the day will grow brighter … and your load lighter

No more anchored to the Ds … instead you will focus on these:

Bright smiles and happy faces to cheer you on in many places,

So do not wait; it is time to celebrate

No longer will your heart be aflutter

Each day you will enjoy lots of fresh-made butter!